This book or parts thereof may not be reproduced in any form, stored in any retrieval system, or transmitted in any form by any means—electronic, mechanical, photocopy, recording, or otherwise— without prior written permission of the publisher or author, except as provided by United States of America copyright law.

978-0-9828831-1-2

Published By WorkingChihuahua Press. All Rights Reserved.

©2024 Mary Oquendo

Hi, I'm Mary,

I began grooming as a second career more than 20 years ago. The groomer I was back then bears little resemblance to the groomer I am today. It has been a long and transformative journey, shaped by my love for animals and an insatiable desire to keep learning. And while I've come far, my education is far from complete. Even now, I dedicate hundreds of hours each year to continuing my education.

All of us are somewhere on our individual grooming paths. And wherever you are on that journey, that's exactly where you need to be. What I envisioned for this book is a guide and reference—not just for those who are starting out, but also for seasoned groomers seeking a gentler, more mindful approach.

My defining moment came because of Pepe, the so-called "evil chihuahua." Pepe had been banned from every local grooming shop when his owner contacted me, desperate for help. She called him her "evil chihuahua"—her words, not mine.

I had been speaking about holistic grooming and the benefits of low-stress handling for years. So I decided to walk my talk and took Pepe on as a client. It took three grooming sessions to turn Pepe from a fear-biting, anxious dog into a calm and cooperative little guy. He had been overwhelmed in noisy shops and had endured rough handling by groomers who just wanted to get the job done quickly.

Pepe became the inspiration behind my first book, Holistic Pet Grooming, co-written with Daryl Conner. It was the first book in the industry to tackle this subject. I am deeply grateful to Barkleigh Productions and Todd Shelley for believing in us and bringing that book to life. (And yes, it's still available at Barkleigh.com!)

The Guide To The **Holistic Pet Grooming System**© is a continuation of everything I've learned and refined over the years.

With gratitude, I dedicate this guide to Barbara Bird and Christein Pearson, early advocates of holistic grooming who helped pave the way during a time when the term was often dismissed or ridiculed.

And to my husband, Ernesto Oquendo—thank you for your unwavering support in every idea and project I dream up. Thanks, Babe.

I don't make recommendations lightly in this book. Every suggestion comes from personal experience or direct knowledge. That's not to say there aren't other—or even better—options out there. I'm simply not personally familiar with them.

The Guide To The Holistic Pet Grooming System©

Introduction: Holistic Pet Grooming System©

On more than one occasion over the past forty years, I've found that a dog or cat has oh-so-carefully aimed and deposited a poop in my grooming smock pocket. And on those occasions, I laughed, though I certainly wasn't happy. I imagine most groomers have days when they question why they do what they do for a living, times that feel a lot like poop-in-a-pocket, but I also know from wonderful experience that this career can bring joy.

I have been grooming dogs and cats since 1984. I've worked in a veterinarian's office, a busy kennel, a cozy grooming shop, and an upscale grooming spa. I have also provided house call grooming and mobile grooming services. I am currently working from my home-based shop, where I plan to keep making pets more beautiful until I can't hold shears anymore. What I have learned over the years is that creating a work environment where all aspects of the job interact cohesively offers the best chance not only for success, but also for a sense of being glad to do my work.

Grooming joyfully can happen, and this guide outlines basic ideas, steps, and plans that an enterprising groomer can use to create a strategy that makes their business work smoothly, safely, and efficiently. This is the basis of making work a happy place to be.

The guide is filled with wonderful information, clear explanations, and even serves as a workbook where readers can absorb the material and then compile their own thoughts and ideas at the end of each chapter to create a personalized guide they can refer back to.

I first met Mary when she was teaching pet first aid classes at a trade show many years ago. I was then, and remain, impressed at the depth of knowledge she possessed about her subject matter. As I got to know her better, I found her to be a consummate professional at any endeavor she tackles. My admiration for her skills in mastering a topic and then presenting the information in a way that makes it marvelously understandable is endless.

This guide is no exception. If you need help in creating a cohesive workspace that runs smoothly and allows you to enjoy the experience, this guide is for you.

Daryl Conner,
Master Pet Stylist, Meritus,
Certified Master Cat Groomer

Table Of Contents

Chapter 1: Holistic Grooming System p. 7

Chapter 2: Pet Layer p. 16

Chapter 3: Client Layer p. 42

Chapter 4: Staff Layer p. 52

Chapter 5: Environment Layer p. 65

Chapter 6: Business Layer p. 78

Chapter 7: Marketing p. 89

Chapter 8: Put It All Together p. 99

Chapter 9: Recommendation List p. 101

Chapter One:

The Holistic Pet Grooming System

Holistic Grooming: A System, Not a Shortcut

Holistic grooming is the sum of many interconnected parts:

There is no one-size-fits-all approach.

Every groomer's version will look different because each of us brings unique experiences, values, and needs to the table. At its core, holistic grooming means considering every facet of your grooming business and making thoughtful adjustments as needed. That includes the pets in your care, the clients who support your work, the staff (including you, the business owner), the atmosphere of your workplace, and the overall health of your business.

What's in a Word?

There, their, and they're. We've all seen how simple words can cause confusion, even when they appear clear on the surface. Now imagine the complexity when a word is more conceptual. Take the word holistic, for example. It's often interpreted differently depending on who's using it. That variance in interpretation is why people sometimes argue over the meaning or value of holistic grooming. Each person is convinced that their understanding is the correct one.

Back in the day, when dinosaurs roamed and online grooming forums reigned, the mere mention of the word holistic could spark ridicule and a heated debate. While we've come a long way in embracing the concept, the term is still frequently misunderstood. The root of the issue lies in how people interpret holistic grooming, rather than how it is defined.

Let's start with the definition.

Whether you spell it holistic or wholistic, the meaning remains the same: it's a theory that systems, especially living systems, are best understood as a whole not as a collection of parts. In other words, the whole is greater than the sum. Applied to business, this means every individual element of your grooming operation influences the entire experience. Your business is not just made up of clients, staff, pets, tools, and tasks, it is the synergy of all of them together.

Traditionally, the holistic model is divided into three key components: **mind, body, and soul**. In the context of your grooming business, I like to think of that third piece as **joy**. When your business operates with mindfulness, physical care, and joy at the center, everything functions more harmoniously.

Understanding this interplay allows you to identify imbalances and address them before they lead to bigger issues. For example, if your building has a carbon monoxide leak due to poor maintenance, the consequences won't stop at a broken heater. That leak could cause health issues for pets, clients, and staff. It might result in behavioral problems, irritability, or even loss of business due to dissatisfied customers. Every issue ripples outward.

From Pieces to a System

It's easy to implement small holistic touches here and there: like adding a break room for employees, switching to energy-efficient lighting, or recycling grooming waste. These are valuable steps. But what if we take it further?

Enter the **Holistic Pet Grooming System©**.

Let's talk about the key term: system. A system is a framework that acknowledges the complexity of interconnected elements; in this case, your grooming business. This includes pets, clients, staff, the physical environment, and the business entity itself. The way these elements interact determines the quality of the grooming experience for everyone involved.

A truly holistic system recognizes that if one area is struggling, it affects all others. But when everything is working in harmony, your business becomes not just functional, but empowered. That's what the **Holistic Pet Grooming System©** is designed to help you achieve.

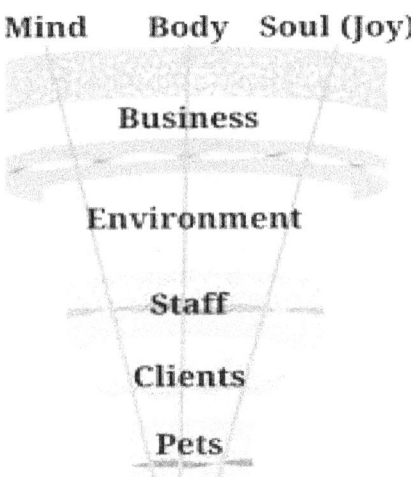

Imagine This. Because I Always Come Back To Food (I'm convinced I was a Labrador in a past life.)

Picture a five-layer birthday cake. Each layer represents a vital part of your grooming business: pets, clients, staff (including you), the environment, and the business itself. Now, insert three sturdy cake dowels to hold it all together; these represent mind, body, and joy (I like to use joy instead of soul).

When everything is in balance, you could flip that cake upside down, and it would stay intact. If someone takes a bite out of one layer, say an issue arises with clients or the environment, the rest of the cake holds steady while you address the problem. But if you ignore it? The structure starts to weaken, and eventually, the entire cake will collapse.

The **Holistic Pet Grooming System**© is built on the idea that when one element is out of sync, it impacts the rest. By keeping a watchful eye on all parts of your system, you can make timely adjustments and maintain the overall integrity and harmony of your business.

It doesn't matter which order you stack your layers (business, pets, clients, staff, environment) they're all essential. What keeps them from toppling over is the foundation of mind, body, and joy working in alignment.

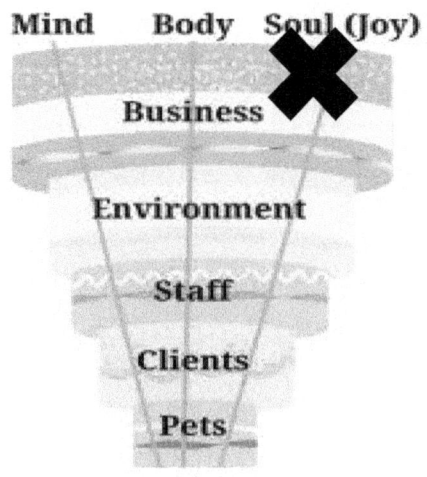

When one of the supports is ignored, the integrity of the whole begins to crumble. The mind and body are forced to carry the weight, straining to compensate for the absence of joy. Remove all three supports, and the entire cake comes crashing down.

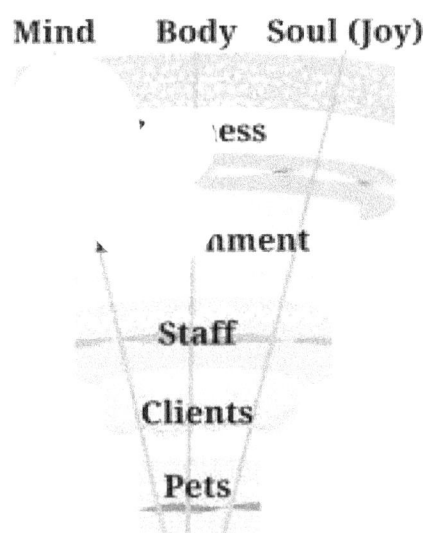

If even one aspect of your business is out of alignment, it can impact everything else.

Let's say you postponed essential maintenance on your grooming van. Now it's broken down and sitting in a repair shop. Since you didn't build a relationship with that shop ahead of time, you're not a priority. You're forced to reschedule appointments. Some clients are understanding, but others are frustrated; a few may not return. Pets go longer between grooms, and you start losing income. On top of that, repairs are expensive. This scenario illustrates how deeply interconnected your business truly is.

However, if you've taken steps to run your business holistically, bouncing back becomes much easier. You've built a relationship with your mechanic, so your van is a higher priority. Your strong rapport with clients means most are willing to wait. You've networked with fellow groomers who can step in and help if needed. You've set aside emergency funds, so you're financially prepared to weather the downtime. Each small decision contributes to a more resilient whole. Here's another example:

Tired, overworked groomers can lead to toxic workplace environments. They might call out frequently or show up with low energy. Pets sense stress hormones and start to act out. That stressed groomer might unintentionally handle the pet more roughly, resulting in poor-quality grooms or even injuries. Clients complain, reviews drop, and the business suffers.

Or this: You've been putting off boiler maintenance. Now there's a carbon monoxide leak, endangering the health and behavior of pets, staff, and clients. Or the icy walkways haven't been cleared, and someone slips and breaks a leg. Suddenly, you're facing injury liability, rescheduled appointments, and lost income.

One thing impacts everything.

When you're aware of how all parts of your business are connected, you can take proactive steps to address issues before they spiral. A holistic approach doesn't just improve your workflow, it strengthens the entire foundation of your business. In any holistic system, the foundation rests on three pillars: mind, body, and soul. Pet grooming is no different. To keep things simple, I'll refer to the "soul" as joy.

The mind shapes the experience: it connects the dots. It's the control center that takes in and processes the information around us. It houses our thoughts, beliefs, emotions, and perceptions. In a grooming business, this includes not only your own mindset, but also that of your pets, staff, clients, and even the energy of your physical space. The mind doesn't function in isolation, it is deeply intertwined with the body and joy. When we become more aware of how these mental elements impact the overall well-being of the **Holistic Pet Grooming System©**, we can make more aligned and compassionate decisions.

The body refers to the physical structure: your salon, home or mobile grooming van, as well as the physical well being of pets, staff, and clients. A strong, healthy body provides the foundation for fulfillment. This includes the condition of skin and coat, a clean and inviting facility, ergonomic tools and furniture, rest areas for staff, and well maintained equipment. When the body is nourished, everything flows more smoothly.

Joy is the heart of it all. It's where happiness, creativity, connection, and meaning reside. It's the dogs that wag their tails when they see you. The clients who trust you without hesitation. The staff who genuinely love what they do. It's what fuels the passion behind the work and reminds you why you started in the first place.

Let's put this into perspective.

In a mobile grooming van: The van itself is the body of the business. The electrical, fuel, and mechanical systems represent the mind, ensuring everything runs as it should. Your pricing, client relationships, and satisfaction reflect the joy—the soul of your business.

Every layer supports the next. You groom pets, manage payments, and maintain your space all within that one environment. Cleanliness, organization, and energy flow through each part of the system.

When one element is off, it impacts the whole. A holistic approach ensures your grooming business isn't just surviving; it's thriving!

"If you are a pet groomer, especially if you've ever thought that the word "Holistic" is some hippy stuff, this is the book for you! It breaks down how everything is connected in an easy-to-follow guide that leaves just enough of the "woo-woo" out to make it absorbable for everyone. A fantastic guide to creating harmony in your grooming shop (and life!), for groomers of all ages and experience levels. So much of this book rang true with my life experiences that I'm looking forward to re-reading and following through with the exercises. Again, Mary gives me homework, and I can't even be mad about it. A valuable addition to any groomer's library." -

Chris Anthony

Chapter Two

The Pet Layer

Let's start with the Pet Layer.

The mind reflects the pet's level of cooperation: how they respond to grooming based on their experiences, emotions, and comfort. The body focuses on their physical needs, including any special care or safety considerations. And joy? That's about understanding what makes the pet truly happy from their perspective.

Consent Grooming: What is it?

As professionals, it's essential that we not only understand but, also, clearly communicate what we mean when we talk about consent grooming.

Consent grooming stands in direct contrast to a "get it done at all costs" mentality. It means giving the pet choice and agency in how they are handled, including the freedom to move away if they choose. While all pets deserve the opportunity for consent grooming, not every pet may require it in the same way.

Cooperative Care focuses on teaching pets how to actively participate in their own grooming and body care needs. It's about building trust and understanding, creating a more collaborative experience between groomer and pet.

Fear Free Grooming is an actionable mindset rooted in both cooperative care and consent. It addresses how to reduce stress in what can be an inherently stressful environment, creating a safer and more positive experience for everyone involved.

Ashley Hanvey has introduced a new concept called Respect

Centered Handling. This approach emphasizes grooming with respect for the pet's physical and emotional well-being. It offers a practical framework for groomers who recognize their handling skills may be outdated and are looking for actionable tools they can implement immediately.

Once groomers recognize the living, sentient being beneath the coat, they often feel inspired to deepen their understanding and better meet each pet's individual needs.

Ideas To Build Trust

It's our responsibility to create that cooperative relationship. It is not the pet's job to accommodate us. You don't build trust by forcing a groom. So, how do you build trust?

You don't force the groom. Take behavior and handling programs. Continually reevaluate what's best for that pet even if that means referring them to someone better suited to their needs.

Cookie visits are another great way to establish familiarity and build trust. In a salon setting, have pet parents bring their pets in for a relaxed "tour" and positive experience—treats, praise, and no pressure. If you're mobile, you can offer meet-and greet visits at the client's home. These short, stress-free introductions allow the pet to associate you and your setup with safety and positivity.

Does this pet have special needs?

Whether the pet is a tripod, arthritic, or has other physical challenges, it's important to adapt your grooming approach with care and compassion. For pets with limited mobility, pool noodles can provide soft, supportive props to help them stay upright, or you may need to allow them to sit or lie on their side during the groom. These pets tire more easily, so it's crucial to watch for signs of fatigue and adjust accordingly.

My geriatric pet owners always received what I lovingly called the "Old Lady Speech" before beginning senior grooming protocols:

"As your pet ages, their grooming needs will change. For some, this may mean less frequent appointments. For others, it may mean more frequent care to stay comfortable. One option is our 'Grooming on the Installment Plan,' where we divide the grooming session into shorter, more manageable visits. While this approach increases the total appointment time, and cost, it greatly benefits your pet's comfort and well-being."

Blind and deaf pets require consistent awareness of your presence. Keeping one hand on the pet throughout the grooming process helps them feel secure and reduces anxiety.

Always know when to stop a groom: your safety and the pet's safety come first. If a situation becomes dangerous, it's your responsibility as the professional to halt the session. Make sure your signed waivers are clear and cover scenarios like this.

Skin and coat grooming is a specialty that requires ongoing education and training. With the right knowledge, you can truly make a difference in the health and comfort of the pets in your care. That said, everyone should have basic knowledge of skin and coat. If you need education, look for programs from Michelle Knowles, Chris Pearson, and Dr. Cliff Faver.

Additional helpful tools include the Groomers' Wall, which offers a safe, solid boundary for pets who need extra stability, especially cats and special-needs animals, and Trach Savers for small pets, regardless of whether they've been diagnosed with tracheal issues.

Cats should be given time to acclimate to the grooming session. In a safe, enclosed area, open the carrier and allow the cat to come out on their own terms. Use this time to calmly set up your grooming and bathing equipment. Keep the carrier door open throughout the session. If the cat becomes startled and bolts, they're far more likely to retreat to the familiar safety of the open carrier rather than attempt to flee the room.

Pets need to feel safe, and that starts before the grooming even begins.

Information Is A Layer of Security

Pet owners should complete all required forms and waivers in advance to ensure a smooth and informed experience.

We've all heard the phrase "Knowledge is power", and when it comes to grooming, having accurate information about a pet before the appointment is essential.

Start with a new client questionnaire. This should be completed in writing, dated, and signed by the pet owner. Key questions to include:

1. **When was your pet's last grooming appointment?**
   This helps you gauge how often the pet is groomed and how familiar they are with the grooming process.
2. **Do you brush your pet at home?**
   Listen without judgment. The pet owner may not be using the correct tools, or may unknowingly be using inexpensive brushes that scratch or hurt the pet. This is a great opportunity to educate them on proper coat maintenance and recommend appropriate equipment.
3. **Has your pet ever bitten anyone?**
   If yes, ask about the circumstances. Context matters, and understanding the situation helps you plan a safer session.
4. **Has your pet ever bitten a groomer?**
   Some pet owners mistakenly believe getting bitten is just part of the groomer's job. It's not. This question reinforces the importance of transparency.
5. **Has your pet ever tried to bite a groomer?**
   A pet that hasn't bitten yet may still attempt to. Knowing this in advance helps you assess potential risk and prepare accordingly.
6. **What medications has your pet taken in the past week?**
   Understanding current medications gives insight into any medical conditions that could impact grooming, such as arthritis, skin issues, or anxiety.

Before you ever put your hands on a pet, all waivers and client information must be completed. Any documents your clients are required to sign should be reviewed by a local business attorney to ensure they are not only legal, but more importantly, enforceable.

Modern client management software makes it easy for clients to complete and sign paperwork in advance of their appointment, helping you stay organized and protected.

Start with Your Terms of Service

Your Terms of Service (ToS) document outlines the conditions under which you accept a pet for grooming. It sets clear expectations for both you and your clients and serves as a foundational agreement. It should include:

Pricing Structure

> Specify whether you charge by breed, coat condition, size, or hourly rate. Clearly list any additional charges, such as de-matting fees, special handling, or add-on services.

Vaccination Requirements

> Outline which vaccinations are required and note if your state mandates specific vaccines that must be kept on file.

Size and Weight Limits

> Define whether you have weight restrictions or size limitations—and be clear about how you measure or categorize them.

Pick-Up and Drop-Off Protocols

State your expected drop-off and pick-up windows. Include any fees for early/late arrivals or extended stays.

Accepted Payment Methods & Due Dates

Clarify which forms of payment you accept and when payment is due—whether at the time of service or by invoice.

No-Show and Cancellation Policies

Define acceptable cancellation timeframes and whether you charge a flat fee or a percentage of the grooming cost for late cancellations or no-shows.

Additional Business Policies

Include anything else important to the way you operate, such as:
- Permission for video or audio recording
- Drop-off instructions
- Policies on aggressive pets, matted coats, or senior pet waivers

This document not only protects your business; it sets the tone for a professional and transparent client relationship.

Collect comprehensive client information.

You should have at least five points of contact for every client. This ensures you can reach them in the event of an emergency or even just to clarify grooming instructions. I recommend including the following signed waivers as part of your client intake forms:

Veterinary Release

Specifies who is financially responsible for any veterinary care in the event of an emergency.

First Aid Release

Grants permission to administer basic first aid in the event of an injury during the grooming process.

CPR Waiver

Authorizes (or declines) the use of CPR if necessary. This is especially important to include, as properly performed CPR can result in broken ribs. In my experience, many senior pet owners choose to opt out of this waiver.

Guardianship Waiver

Covers situations in which you may need to assume temporary guardianship of a pet during a disaster or emergency, until the owner is able to reclaim them.

You can also establish aggressive pet policies, matted coat policies, and senior pet care policies to clearly outline expectations, procedures, and additional fees or considerations related to each situation.

Recording Policy

If you record any part of your grooming process—video or audio—be consistent and transparent. If you tell clients you record sessions, then be sure you actually do. If a dispute arises and you claim to have footage but can't produce it, the client may assume you're hiding something. It's better to either commit to recording or clearly state that you don't.

What Are Your Terms Of Service?

Once the pet has arrived for their appointment, but before any grooming begins, you must ensure the pet is healthy enough to groom.

Always Perform a Pet Assessment Before Every Groom!

Your assessment should include the following:

Observe the pet walking.
   Look for signs of limping, stiffness, or lethargy.

Check their tracking.
   Walk in front of the pet and ensure they follow your movement with their eyes. As you pass, check for any discharge from the eyes or nose, especially in cats, as feline respiratory infections are highly contagious.

Initial touch should be from the rear.
   The first time you lay hands on a pet, start from the

rear end. If a simple touch triggers a bite response, this gives you time to react and safely back away.

Palpate the body.
Gently run your hands over the pet's body, noting any lumps, sensitivity, or changes in body language. Pets know where it hurts, and they will often let you know.

Check the ears.
Feel for heat or look for discharge, both of which could indicate an underlying medical issue.

Inspect the gums. This is critical!
Healthy gums should be bubblegum pink. Any deviation could be a sign of a serious medical condition:
- Red gums may indicate poisoning or heatstroke.
- Pale gums suggest poor circulation.
- Blue or purple gums can signal hypoxia or tracheal issues.
- Yellow gums may point to liver failure.

Examine the teeth.
Dental disease is painful. Imagine having a toothache and then using an electric toothbrush—that's essentially what clipping near the face feels like for a pet in pain. Pets with bad teeth are often protective of their face and may react during grooming.

Assess the legs and belly.
Run your hands down the legs and under the belly.

If the abdomen is hard and distended, this is an emergency requiring immediate veterinary attention. Also check for mammary tumors, and conclude your assessment with the genital and anal areas.

Document all findings.

Note any abnormalities on the intake form, but avoid diagnosing. Instead of saying, "Your pet has an ear infection," describe what you observe: "Your pet's ears feel warm and there's a black discharge present."

Feline Body Map

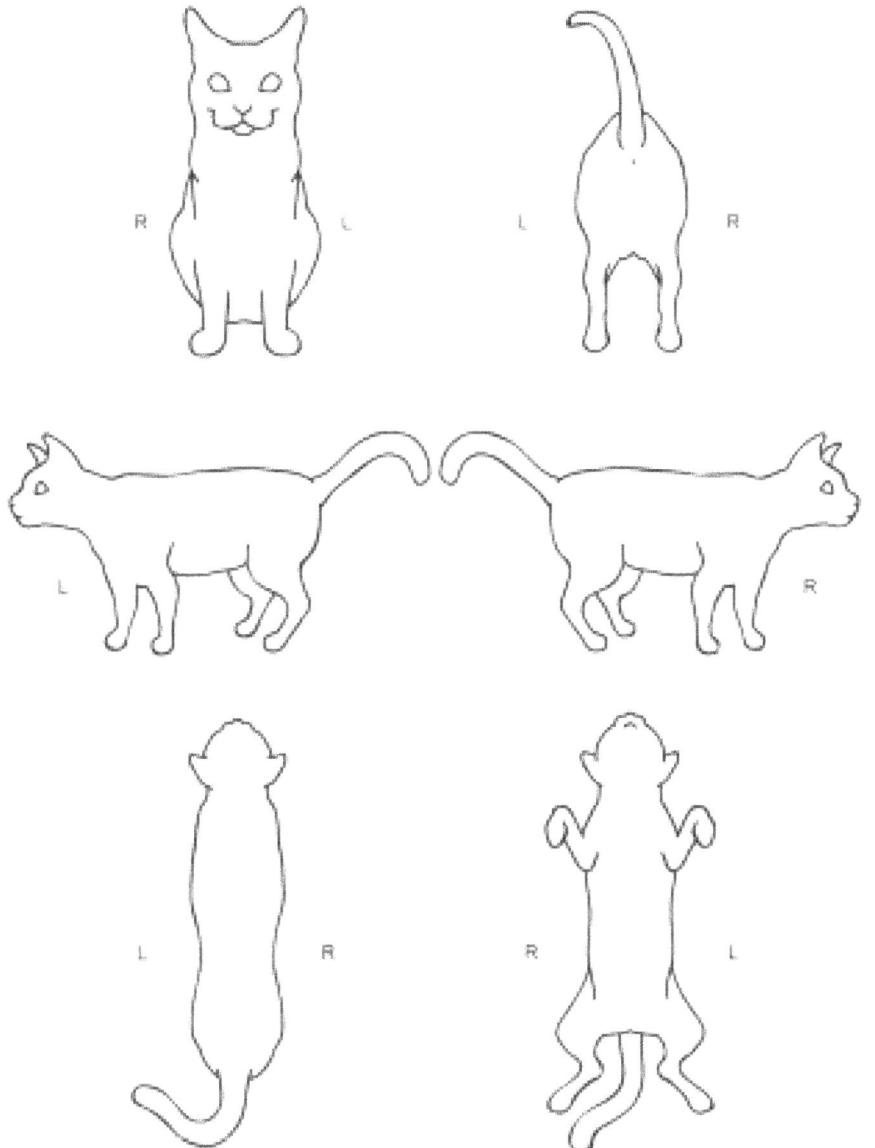

Notes:

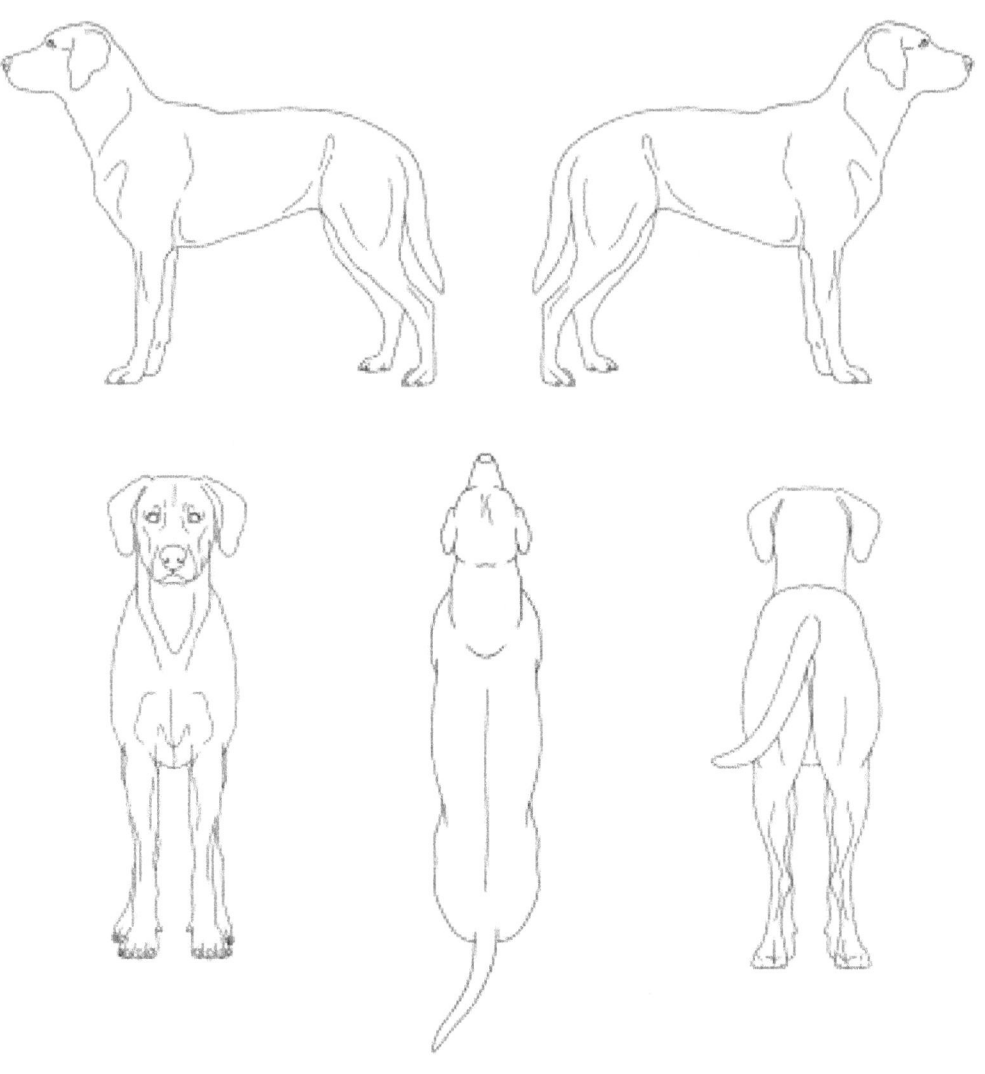

Notes:
_____
_____
_____
_____
_____
_____
_____

Injuries happen. Sometimes they zig, we zag and, suddenly, there's blood. First and foremost, stay calm. Take a deep breath and assess the situation. Ensure the pet is safe and retrieve your pet first aid kit.

If the pet is in pain, or if movement is likely to cause pain, muzzle and restrain them appropriately. Whenever possible, enlist a second pair of hands to help stabilize the pet and ensure everyone's safety.

Image below: Clean the wound using a pet-safe wound cleanser. Elevate the injured area above the heart and apply direct pressure with non-stick gauze to help control bleeding.

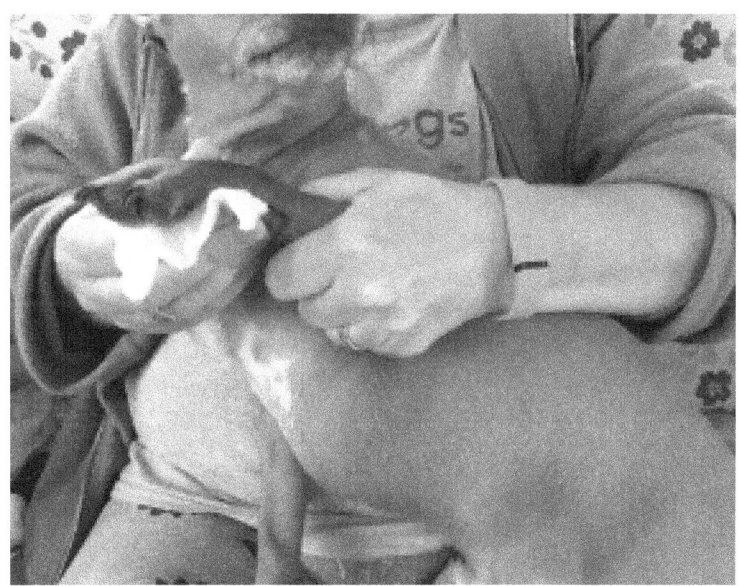

Image below: Wrap the injury securely and contact the pet's owner. If necessary, transport the pet to a veterinarian for further care.

It's essential to refresh your skills regularly; take a hands-on pet first aid course at least once a year. I highly recommend Pet Tech for comprehensive, professional training.

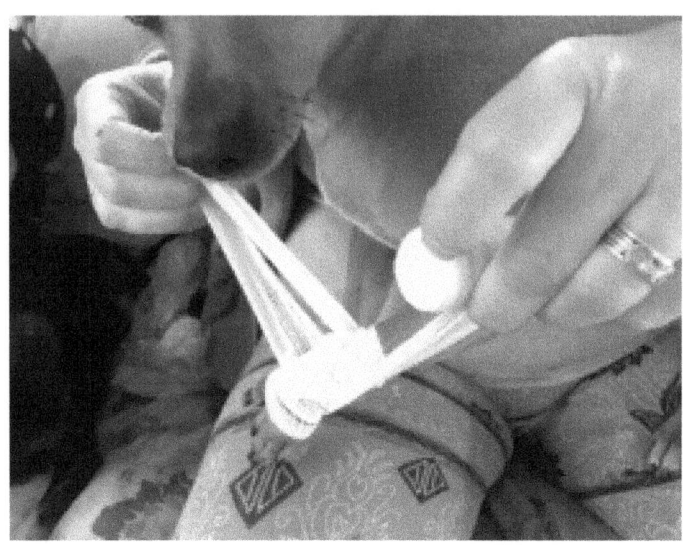

What happens if a pet dies in your care?

1. Immediately contact a veterinarian and transport the pet to their office. You should already have a signed veterinary release from the owner.

2. Request a necropsy report. Be aware that the report is given to the person who orders and pays for it. Do not assume the owner will share it with you.

3. Contact the owner as soon as possible. Inform them that there has been an incident and that you will meet them at the veterinary office.

4. Prepare a social media statement. This should already be part of your prewritten crisis communication scripts. Be

factual, brief, and compassionate.

5. Debrief your staff. A loss can be traumatic for your team, and they may need time and support to process it. Consider offering access to grief counseling or peer support resources.

Tips for Safer, More Compassionate Grooming

Know when to refer. Recognize when a pet's needs are better served by another groomer with specialized experience or equipment.

Use quick-release grooming loops. Every grooming loop should have a quick-release mechanism for safety.

Invest in safety tools. Products like the Groomer's Wall and Trach Savers from All4Groomers are essential for supporting safe and effective handling.

Take a behavior and handling class. For dogs, consider courses from Ashley Hanvey, Melissa Jepson, Michelle Knowles, or Mary Kniskern. For cats, look into training with myself or Anjie Coates. These classes cover safe muzzling, handling, and restraint techniques.

Create a low-stress environment for cats. Consider scheduling cat-only days or designating a separate cat grooming room to reduce stress and overstimulation.

Minimize visual triggers. Be mindful of pets walking past others on grooming tables, as it can cause anxiety or reactivity. Limit reception area traffic.

Only allow one pet at a time in the reception area to prevent unnecessary stress or altercations.

PET FIRST AID KIT

- [ ] Bandaids
- [ ] Vetericyn
- [ ] Antibiotic Cream
- [ ] Non-stick Gauze
- [ ] Gauze Pads
- [ ] Gauze Rolls
- [ ] Vet Wrap
- [ ] Sam Splint
- [ ] Hydrogen Peroxide
- [ ] Squirt Bottle
- [ ] Antihistamine
- [ ] Safety Pin
- [ ] Black Tea Bag
- [ ] Sanitary Napkin
- [ ] Plastic Wrap
- [ ] Plastic Baggies
- [ ] Expired Plastic Gift Card

What Makes a Pet Happy?

Just as important as all the physical information is the pet's happiness. Happiness looks different for every pet, and as a professional groomer, it's your job to discover what brings each one joy. These little joys should be factored into your pricing structure, as they take time, effort, and personalization.

Be sure to note the pet's specific joy on their information card. It helps you create a consistent, positive experience tailored to their needs.

General Tips:

All pets appreciate routine. Predictability helps reduce stress. Knowing what to expect builds trust, so keep surprises to a minimum.

Know when to pause or stop the groom. If a pet becomes overstimulated or agitated, a short break can make all the difference in maintaining cooperation.

Joys I've Seen Over the Years:

<u>Accessories.</u>

> Some pets love finishing touches. My dog Kira didn't feel complete without a fancy collar. Ozzie, a large German Shepherd who lived in a construction office, proudly strutted around showing off his bandana to the crew.

Toys.

A simple squeaky toy or cheap stuffed animal can be a big hit.

Treats.

For mobile clients, I gave treats after the groom, usually inside the home. I've been dragged to many a front door by eager dogs! Jet, a black lab, went from bucking bronco to calm client the moment he realized Slim Jims were involved.

Belly rubs.

Never underestimate the value of a good belly rub as a reward or stress reliever.

Putting on a show.

Some dogs are natural performers. They act out in front of their owners, but the moment that door closes, they settle down and happily enjoy the groom. It's all part of the act!

When pets are in balance, they trust us. We meet their needs, and they understand there's a reward waiting for them at the end of the groom. This sense of balance creates a happy, cooperative pet, and the positive, energetic shift it brings radiates throughout the entire facility, influencing every layer of the grooming experience.

It's essential to recognize when a pet is out of balance. Some pets don't just "put on a show" for their owners, they remain scared even after the owners leave. These pets are more likely to be uncooperative, and fear often increases the risk of biting.

Uncooperative pets can lead to stressed groomers, rushed or sloppy grooms, unhappy clients, negative reviews, and a higher risk of injury to the pet.

Just as a balanced pet creates positive ripple effects across all layers of the grooming experience, an imbalanced or fearful pet can cause a negative energetic shift that impacts the entire environment. Recognizing and addressing these imbalances is key to maintaining a safe, successful grooming space.

Continuing education should cover key areas such as behavior and handling, skin and coat care, pet first aid, safety and health protocols, and breed-specific grooming techniques.

Many instructors offer in-person training at industry trade shows and are often willing to travel for private workshops or seminars. Additionally, most are available for online instruction, making it easier than ever to invest in your professional growth.

To create the necessary forms and scripts, my recommendation is to contact Denise Heroux or Anjie Coates.

Joy List Ideas

Ideas For The Terms of Service

Create The Following For This Layer

- **Health Acknowledgement Form**
- **Client Intake Forms**
- **Senior Waivers**
- **First Aid, CPR, Veterinary, and Guardianship Waivers**
- **New Client Questionnaire**
- **Aggressive Pet Waiver**
- **Matting Releases**
- **Terms Of Service**
- **Pre-prepared Scripts**
- **Invoice/Receipts**
- **Report Cards**
- **Specific Terms Of Service For Cats**
- **Nose To Tail Assessment Form**

What Immediate Changes Can You Make For This Layer

Continuing Education

Chapter Three

The Client Layer

Let's Talk About Clients.

Continually marketing to new clients can be costly. That's why it's so important to focus on retaining the right ones: happy, balanced clients who stay with us, respect our boundaries, and refer others like them. While attracting new clients has its place, building strong, lasting relationships with satisfied clients is often the more sustainable and joyful path.

When we think about the joy in this layer of business, it's not just about keeping clients; it's about keeping the right clients. Not everyone will be a good fit, and that's okay. We want to create an experience that resonates with those who align with our values, so we can continue doing the work we love with people who truly appreciate it.

It all starts with educated clients. Educated clients are good clients.

Begin with professionalism.

It's more than just wearing a uniform; it's a mindset. You should consistently project competence and confidence in your craft. This includes showcasing your qualifications, certificates displayed on your shop wall, organized in a binder, or listed on your website.

Remember, you determine the grooming options available, not the client. Conduct thorough nose-to-tail assessments with the pet owners, and clearly explain when their requests aren't feasible and why. Address potential concerns early—before they become problems.

Have educational handouts ready on common topics like matting, senior pet care, behavioral changes, and frequently asked questions (FAQ's). Proactively opening a nonjudgmental dialogue sets the tone for trust and cooperation.

Use tools like coat length charts and even offer an equipment loaner program to support pet owners at home. Demonstrate how to use grooming tools correctly, and if you don't sell retail products, guide them on where to find the right equipment.

Education builds trust, and trust builds long-term, respectful client relationships.

You uphold your boundaries through signed, legally reviewed paperwork. Documents that have been evaluated by a business attorney licensed in your state to ensure enforceability and compliance.

Professionalism Also Means Good Boundaries

Verbal abuse from clients is never acceptable. If a situation escalates, be prepared to contact the appropriate authorities, whether it's the non-emergency police line or 911, based on the severity of the behavior. Aggressive or threatening clients should be handled by professionals trained for those situations.

Familiarize yourself with your state's criminal code regarding non-payment, so you understand your rights and options. Practice how you'll handle these scenarios through role-play exercises, either with your staff or, if you're a solo operator, by collaborating with fellow shop owners.

Clear boundaries protect your business, your team, and your peace of mind.

What makes a client happy?

Just like the pets in our care, client happiness varies from person to person. Sometimes, ensuring a client's happiness means recognizing they may be better suited to a different groomer; perhaps one who offers a niche service or is simply a better fit for their expectations, especially if they've shown a lack of respect for your business.

One simple way to gauge client satisfaction is through a short, two-question survey. Clients appreciate when their opinions are valued. Start with a positive: "What do you love about our business?" Look for repeated phrases, these become your marketing keywords when attracting new clients. The second question should be constructive: "What would you change about our business?" Patterns in responses will highlight areas for improvement, though most feedback is often minor and easily addressed.

Consider small gestures that build client goodwill. Could you give them a treat? A colleague of mine, whose shop is in a remote area, offers homemade baked goods in the waiting area.

You could also host an exclusive event for your top clients (be transparent about how to earn an invite). My local pet store does this annually, complete with a generous spread, and every time, I end up happily spending more than I intended.

Make sure your space is clean and pleasant-smelling, it sends a clear message that you prioritize sanitation and care.

Other thoughtful touches include:
- Featuring client pets on Instagram or TikTok.
- Offering consignment space for artistic clients to showcase their creations.
- Providing assistance for disabled or senior clients bringing in pets.

Client happiness is built on attention, appreciation, and the little things that show you care.

Happy clients refer their friends and family, and they'll even tell you which referrals deserve a spot on your schedule. These clients respect your policies, show up with a smile at drop-off and pick-up, and genuinely appreciate the care you provide.

What makes a client imbalanced?

Before we dive into what an imbalanced client looks like, remember this, not everyone is meant to be your client. If the issue can't be resolved, or they're unwilling to make changes, it's okay to let them go. Keeping them comes at a cost.

These clients create a ripple effect throughout your business, impacting staff morale, the work environment, and ultimately, your bottom line.

Imbalanced clients often require constant adjustments, are verbally abusive, delay or avoid payments, show up late for drop-off or pick-up, cancel at the last minute, and are quick to threaten or leave negative reviews. No matter what you do, they're unlikely to ever be satisfied.

Ask yourself, how much time are you spending trying to appease them versus what you're earning from them?

In some cases, a candid, respectful conversation can shift the dynamic and turn them into good clients. But be prepared to part ways and make room for someone who truly aligns with your business values.

Do not hesitate to contact law enforcement if you are dealing with abusive or threatening clients. When reporting non-payment through a non-emergency line, it's helpful to be prepared: research and have the criminal code for non-payment in your state readily available. You can find this information by searching "criminal code non-payment+ [your state]" online.

Additionally, for your safety, consider conducting a background check before entering a client's home. You can search public sex offender registries by county and state to ensure you are not unknowingly walking into a potentially dangerous situation.

Seek out continuing education in customer service, client communication, and business policy. In addition to pet industry educators, there's a wealth of free, high-quality resources available through www.sba.gov and www.score.org to help strengthen your business skills and client relations.

Joy List Ideas

Create The Following For This Layer

- Calendar Of Events
- What To Expect Handout
- QR codes Linked To Review Sites
- Customer Service Scripts
- Survey

What Immediate Changes Can You Make For This Layer

Continuing Education

Chapter Four

The Staff Layer

"But I don't have any staff."

Actually, you do.

Even if you're a solo groomer, you are the staff. This layer of the **Holistic Grooming System©** focuses on the humans within your business, whether that's a full team or just you.

Why should you care if you (or your team) are happy? After all, it's a business, and getting paid should be enough, right? Not quite. Here's why happiness matters:

1. Pets can smell happiness.
    Animals are incredibly intuitive. They can pick up on your emotional state. Happy endorphins are contagious, just like stress and frustration.

2. Happy groomers stay.
    Whether it's you or your staff, job satisfaction reduces turnover and keeps your business running smoothly.

3. Positive energy is powerful.
    Happy, engaged groomers create a sense of camaraderie and flow. That energy radiates throughout your space, and every pet and client will feel it.

4. Unhappy groomers burn out.
    Burnout is a common topic in grooming forums for a reason. Neglecting your emotional well-being will eventually affect your work, your health, and your

business.

Whether you're a solo operator or managing a team, your well-being is not a luxury, it's a foundational piece of a thriving grooming business.

It all starts with the mind. Ask yourself: Are you truly meeting the mental and emotional needs of your team? Are they lazy or are they simply assigned to the wrong tasks for your business?

For example, an introverted, non-confrontational groomer may struggle with assertive client interactions. Forcing them into that role can lead to stressful encounters and even client conflicts. Instead, consider assigning these team members to back-end tasks like admin work or cleaning, while more assertive employees handle the front end client communication. Better yet, hire a receptionist if the budget allows.

Do some employees dread coming to work because of ongoing drama? Invest in conflict resolution and de-escalation training to help manage and prevent workplace tension.

It's also important to recognize that our industry attracts a significantly higher percentage of individuals from the neurodiverse community. "Diverse" is the key word: they can each learn, process, and respond differently. What makes perfect sense to a neurotypical person might not translate at all to a neurodiverse employee. Fortunately, there are excellent workshops available that address how to support neurodiverse team members in professional environments.

Lastly, do you have a structured and supportive onboarding process for new hires? Starting with the right foundation ensures better long-term success—for both your employees and your business.

Take Care of The Body (Yours and Theirs)

Are you providing your team with ergonomic tools and equipment to support their physical well-being? Are you ensuring they take regular lunch breaks and rest periods? Working eight hours straight without a break is not a badge of honor—it's a recipe for burnout. Our bodies aren't built to endure that kind of strain without proper recovery time.

Next consider your onboarding process: Is it structured in a way that supports the physical and emotional adjustment of new employees?

Finally, ask yourself: Do your staff members have time off for vacations, family functions, and personal needs? Rest and time away are essential for long-term health, productivity, and job satisfaction.

Sample Employee Wellness Policy

This <u>Employee Wellness Policy</u> is designed to support the physical, mental, and emotional well-being of all staff members. A healthy and supported team is essential to the success of our grooming business and the quality of care we provide to pets and their owners.

   1. Physical Wellness

All staff will have access to ergonomic tools and equipment to reduce physical strain and promote comfort during grooming tasks.
> • Scheduled lunch and rest breaks are mandatory. Employees are encouraged to take short, regular breaks to rest and recharge.
> • Employees are provided with time off for vacations, family obligations, and personal days to maintain a healthy work life balance.

2. Mental And Emotional Wellness
   Staff are encouraged to communicate openly about stressors or challenges they face on the job.
   > • Resources and training will be made available on topics such as conflict resolution, de-escalation, and handling stress.
   > • The workplace culture will prioritize respect, collaboration, and emotional safety.

3. Neurodiversity And Inclusive Learning
   We recognize and value the diversity of learning styles and cognitive differences within our team.
   > • Training and onboarding processes will be adapted to support both neurotypical and neurodiverse employees.
   > • Staff will be provided access to relevant workshops and educational resources to support inclusive teamwork.

4. Onboarding Support
    A structured onboarding process will be in place to ensure new employees are supported and set up for success.
    • New hires will be given time to acclimate to the workflow, expectations, and physical demands of the job.

5. Continuous Improvement
    This policy will be reviewed regularly and updated as needed to reflect best practices in employee wellness.
    • Staff feedback is encouraged and valued in shaping future wellness initiatives.

Providing Joy in the Workplace

One of the most meaningful ways to create joy for your groomers is by ensuring they earn a living wage. If your business is struggling to make that possible, I strongly recommend working with a business coach who can help you restructure and grow in a sustainable way that benefits both you and your team.

Are you encouraging your groomers to pursue continuing education? I left the corporate world because I was expected to invest in my own professional development, training that directly benefited the company's bottom line, without support or recognition. I was also discouraged from attending trade shows, even though I was one of the region's top-producing groomers. Eventually, I attended a show on my own time and dime. While there, I put a deposit down on a mobile grooming van. This changed the trajectory of my career. I left corporate because I didn't feel appreciated.

Joy at work isn't just about money: it's about respect, recognition, and opportunity. Our industry also has a deeply emotional side. When we lose pets, the grief can be overwhelming. Bringing in a grief counselor or providing resources for emotional support shows your team that their feelings matter.

And let's not forget: joy can be compromised by toxic workplace culture. Some groomers find satisfaction in belittling or bullying others, but that behavior has no place in a healthy work environment. Ask yourself: Do you want a "mean girls" club, or a supportive, empowered team?

To build connection and camaraderie:
- ❖ Hold monthly staff meetings to foster open communication.
- ❖ Plan fun team-building activities like paint-and-sip nights, glass-cutting workshops, or escape rooms.

A joyful workplace is a thriving workplace. Make it your mission to create one.

Joy Ideas

How To Create A Balanced Workplace

A positive balanced workplace culture is the foundation of a thriving grooming business. It influences how employees interact with one another, how they treat clients and pets, and how they feel about their work. Creating an intentional, supportive, and respectful culture leads to better teamwork, improved client satisfaction, and overall business success.

1. Emotional Environment

- When staff is in balance, happy endorphins flood the business. Pets can sense this positive energy and respond calmly and cooperatively.
- Clients walk into a cheerful environment, which builds trust and encourages repeat business.
- A happy workplace leads to a happy business owner— problems are addressed quickly and effectively thanks to well-defined processes.

2. Respect And Inclusion

- Every team member deserves respect, regardless of their role or background.
- Promote an inclusive culture that values neurodiversity, learning styles, and different communication needs.
- Zero tolerance for bullying, gossip, or exclusionary behavior. A safe and respectful space benefits everyone.

3. Team Bonding And Communication

- Hold monthly staff meetings to foster communication, address concerns, and celebrate successes.
- Encourage open, judgment-free dialogue between staff and management.
- Organize occasional team-building activities like paint-and sip events, escape rooms, or casual get-togethers to strengthen camaraderie.

4. Recognition And Support

- Acknowledge hard work and achievements regularly. Recognition boosts morale and motivates performance.
- Provide emotional support during difficult times, such as pet loss, through grief counseling or peer support options.
- Support continued education and professional growth as part of your investment in each team member's future.

Let's talk about staff turnover.

Even in a healthy work environment, some employee turnover is expected. Groomers may leave to start their own businesses or pursue opportunities that better align with their goals. That's normal.

However, high turnover is a major red flag, it's often the clearest sign of imbalance within your business. When employees consistently leave, it's time to take a closer look at your workplace culture, leadership, and support systems.

Recommend continuing education on topics including: grief support, ergonomics, employee management, workplace safety and health, supporting neurodiverse employees, and basic human first aid.

Create The Following For This Layer

- List Of Well Stocked Breakroom
- Monthly Meeting (Even if its just you) Schedule
- Continuing Education

What Immediate Changes Can You Make For This Layer

Continuing Education

Chapter Five

The Environment Layer

The Environment Layer: Caring for Your Four Walls

This layer of the **Holistic Grooming System**© focuses on the well-being of your physical workspace—the atmosphere, energy, and safety within your grooming environment.

The Mind of the Environment: Creating a Safe Space

Your workspace should be a safe space, not only for pets but for the humans who work there. That means protecting your team from workplace drama, abusive clients, and unsafe situations.

Know when a situation escalates to the point where you need to call 911. Remember, you have a legal obligation to keep employees safe from known risks, including harassment and unsafe conditions.

Set clear expectations for grooming procedures, maintenance routines, and sanitation protocols and document these in your employee manual.

Be transparent about employee meetings and invite open dialogue. Reflect on your leadership role. If dissatisfaction is recurring among staff, it may require some honest introspection and a willingness to adapt.

Problems within the work environment don't stay contained, they often spill into your employees' personal lives, impacting their well-being outside of work. Prioritizing a healthy environment is essential for long-term success and staff retention.

The Body of The Environment: The Physical Elements

The body of your grooming environment is all about the physical elements—both the hard and soft products that influence the daily well-being of your staff and the pets in your care.

Hard Products

These include ergonomic equipment such as grooming tables, mats, tubs, chairs, and scissors. Each one directly impacts the musculoskeletal health of your team. Ask yourself:

- Is the workspace well-organized?
- Are tools and supplies easy to access and ergonomic?

Good organization reduces strain, increases efficiency, and contributes to a safer, more comfortable environment.

Let's talk about why <u>ergonomics</u> is so important.

Grooming is a physically demanding profession. Maintaining good health is far easier than trying to repair years of damage later in life. It's never too late to start making better choices. But it all starts with ergonomics.

What Is <u>Ergonomics</u>?

Ergonomics is the science of adapting a job to fit the worker.

The goal in using the right products is to reduce or eliminate musculoskeletal disorders (MSDs). MSDs affect the muscles, tendons, ligaments, nerves, vertebrae, blood vessels, and bones, essentially, the body's movement system.

Examples of Common Musculoskeletal Disorders (MSDs):

- Carpal Tunnel Syndrome
- Epicondylitis
- de Quervain's Syndrome
- Degenerative Disc Disease
- Digital Neuritis
- Herniated Disc
- Ligament, Muscle, or Tendon Strain
- Rotator Cuff Tendonitis
- General Tendonitis
- Trigger Finger or Thumb
- Ruptured Disc

Fact: According to the U.S. Bureau of Labor, MSDs account for nearly 30% of all workers' compensation claims, averaging $15,000 per case.

How MSDs Develop

Muscles become fatigued due to repeated use. Without adequate recovery, this fatigue leads to chronic strain. Over time, this cycle creates lasting damage.

Contributing Risk Factors

Poor personal health habits often contribute to MSDs. Here's how to reduce risk:

✖ Smoking
→ Increases risk for MSDs and many chronic illnesses. Consider one of the many modern cessation tools.

✖ Excessive Alcohol Consumption
→ Damages the liver, impacting the body's ability to fight inflammation. Limit intake and hydrate between drinks.

✖ Inadequate Sleep
→ Disrupts hormone balance and organ function. Try going to bed at the same time nightly and limit screen time beforehand.

✖ Inflammatory Diet
→ Reduce intake of sugar, caffeine, trans fats, omega-6 oils, refined carbs, MSG, gluten, casein, and artificial sweeteners.

✖ Dehydration
→ Harms organ function. Drink half your body weight in ounces of water daily.

✖ Lack of Exercise
→ Weak muscles increase fatigue and recovery time. Regular movement strengthens your entire system.

✖ Obesity
→ Excess weight puts strain on the entire musculoskeletal system.

Work-Related Risk Factors:

! Highly Repetitive Tasks
→ Actions like scissoring, brushing, and clipping create fatigue.

- ✓ Take frequent breaks.
- ✓ Use ergonomically fitted tools.
- ✓ Attend trade shows to test equipment and learn proper usage.

! Forceful Exertions
→ Lifting heavy dogs or equipment improperly leads to injury.
- ✓ Use ramps, electric tables, and ask for help.

! Awkward Postures
→ Working at incorrect heights strains your body.
- ✓ Adjust table height.
- ✓ Raise small pets in tubs.
- ✓ Move around the pet instead of bending unnaturally.

! Vibrating Tools
→ Prolonged use can lead to conditions like Raynaud's disease.
- ✓ Test clippers for vibration at trade shows.
- ✓ Ask manufacturers for data on vibration levels.
- ✓ Take breaks during extended clipper use.

! Sustained Postures
→ Staying in one position too long (sitting or

standing) is harmful.
- ✔️ Alternate between sitting and standing.
- ✔️ Invest in restaurant-grade anti-fatigue mats.
  - 📍 Bonus Tip: Invest in Quality Shoes
- ✔️ Choose shoes based on your arch type (neutral, low, or high).
- ✔️ Visit a specialty shoe store for a proper fit.

The earlier you start implementing healthy lifestyle and work habits, the easier it becomes to prevent or reverse damage.

Soft Products

What about the products you apply to the pets themselves? Do you know what's actually in them?

Be cautious of greenwashing: marketing that uses eco friendly language without real therapeutic value. Currently, no state or federal agency regulates how products intended for topical use on pets are labeled. It's up to you to research and verify their safety and efficacy.

Bringing Joy to the Environment

Joy in the grooming space isn't just about mood, it can have real effects on behavior, performance, and perception.

Here are a few ways to elevate the energy in your space:

Temperature:

Something as simple as maintaining a comfortable temperature for both pets and bathers can make a big difference in how everyone feels.

Aromatherapy:

Use caution—what's pleasant for humans may be overwhelming for pets, especially cats. Cats may have difficulty processing essential oils, even in diluted or indirect forms. When in doubt, skip the scents or opt for truly pet-safe options.

Color:

Color psychology is a powerful design tool. Fast food chains often use reds, oranges, and yellows to stimulate appetite and encourage quick turnover. High-end restaurants favor blues and browns to promote relaxation and a lingering experience.

Do a deep dive into color psychology; Madison Avenue certainly has. Look at your own spending habits and note which colors you're naturally drawn to. Apply this knowledge to your space intentionally.

Music:

My favorite music to play in my mobile grooming van was Steven Halpern's Chakra Suite; it had a calming effect on both myself and the pets. Today, you can easily find music designed for pets through platforms like Amazon, YouTube, Spotify, and iTunes. Experiment to find what works best for your space and the pets in your care.

Plants:

Plants can be a wonderful addition to any grooming environment! They help purify the air and bring a sense of calm and natural beauty. However, use caution if you have shop cats, as some plants can be toxic to them.

In my mobile grooming van, I kept a few plants on board. During travel, I would place them in the tub for safety, and at the end of the day, I returned them to a spot where they could receive proper sunlight. It was a simple ritual that brought life and freshness into the space.

You know this layer is balanced when you walk into your space feeling clean, calm, and happy. There's a sense of order, the air is fresh, your tools are ready, and you greet the day with a smile.

When this layer is neglected, things begin to break down (literally and energetically):

- Equipment frequently malfunctions
- Injuries occur due to damaged blades or poor ergonomics
- Pets seem to have more frequent skin issues
- The facility never feels fully clean or may even develop an unpleasant odor

These are warning signs that your physical environment needs attention. To support this layer, include the following topics in your ongoing training:

- OSHA compliance and safety standards
- Emergency and disaster planning
- Basic self-defense training for personal safety in the workplace

What Immediate Changes Can You Make For This Layer

What Needs To Be Created For This Layer

- **Emergency And Disaster Manual**
- **Standard Operating Manual**
- **Employee Manual**

Continuing Education

Chapter Six

The Business Layer

Mind, Body, and Joy: The Core of Your Business

In your business, the mind is represented by your organization and operating systems.

The body is the physical space: whether that's a grooming salon, mobile van, or the vehicle you use for house calls.

And the joy is found in your profit and growth.

The Mind: Systems and Structure

Organization is more than just knowing where your supplies and forms are stored. It's about having efficient systems in place that streamline every aspect of your operations. This includes:

- Business software for accounting, scheduling, payroll, and client management
- Automation tools that reduce manual tasks and save time
- Regular reviews of schedules, policies, and procedures to ensure they still serve your business
- Developing leadership skills to help you determine when to stand firm and when to be flexible

The Body: Physical and Operational Maintenance

For brick-and-mortar salons, this means consistent facility maintenance, cleanliness, and organization. For house call groomers, this layer becomes more complex. Ask yourself:

- What vehicle do you use to transport your equipment?
- How well-organized is your setup to minimize what you need to

carry into each home?
- Are you maintaining your vehicle, equipment, and inventory systems regularly?

For mobile groomers, this includes both the interior and exterior of the grooming van, as well as all mechanical systems. Don't overlook safety measures such as:

★ Fire extinguishers
★ Carbon monoxide detectors
★ Smoke alarms
★ Also, have a designated, accessible place to store important manuals and Standard Operating Procedures (SOPs).

The Joy: Profit, Purpose, and Growth

What truly brings a business joy?

At its core, financial success is essential. Your business should not only generate profit, but also ensure:

➢ Your employees are fairly compensated
➢ You, as the business owner, enjoy a sustainable livelihood

But joy goes beyond the numbers. Consider your growth trajectory.

➢ Are you expanding in a way that stays true to your mission and values?
➢ Are you nurturing a culture that encourages innovation, teamwork, and integrity?

True joy in business is a harmonious blend of:

- Financial stability
- Engaged, supported employees
- Ethical, values-driven growth

When all three layers, mind, body, and joy, are in balance, your business doesn't just function; it flourishes.

Balance vs. Burnout: A Tale of Two Businesses

A well-balanced business is marked by low employee and client turnover, a clear indicator of a healthy, supportive work environment. In this kind of workplace, employees feel valued, engaged, and empowered, which naturally leads to strong client relationships rooted in loyalty and trust.

Business owners in these environments play a pivotal role. They prioritize staff well-being, foster a positive culture, and genuinely look forward to coming to work. They recognize the critical importance of mental health and work-life balance, not just for their team, but for themselves. Taking time off, including vacations, isn't seen as a luxury but as a necessary investment in sustained productivity and creativity.

By encouraging breaks and prioritizing self-care, these business owners ensure that both employees and clients feel appreciated, respected, and invested in. This intentional culture of wellness and accountability becomes a foundation for long-term success.

In contrast, a struggling business often faces a very different reality.

High turnover, among both staff and clients, signals a deep imbalance. The business owner may feel overwhelmed, isolated, and disillusioned, questioning why they ever started in the first place. Despite working 60–80+ hours a week, they remain caught in a cycle of financial instability, unable to enjoy the fruits of their labor.

Vacations become a distant memory, personal life suffers, and burnout sets in. Instead of addressing internal issues, the owner may begin to blame external factors, making statements like:

"I can't catch a break."
"Nobody wants to work anymore."
"I hate my clients."

These sentiments reflect more than frustration. They signal emotional exhaustion and a loss of purpose. This cycle of blame, stress, and disconnection doesn't just harm the business—it harms the people within it.

The solution lies in introspection, accountability, and a willingness to change. Real transformation starts when business owners begin to ask tough questions, seek support, and commit to building a healthier, more intentional path forward.

Take Back Your Business

To strengthen your grooming business, consider expanding your knowledge in the following areas:

- ❖ Leadership and team management

- ❖ Sanitation and infection control
- ❖ Emergency and disaster planning
- ❖ Pricing strategies and profitability
- ❖ General business education
- ❖ Holistic pet care practices

Take advantage of free resources at www.SBA.gov and www.Score.org for expert guidance and business tools.

And when you're ready to level up, invest in a qualified business coach to help you build and sustain long-term success.

Consider a Virtual Assistant (VA)

Running a pet business, whether it's grooming, training, daycare, retail, or pet sitting, comes with more responsibilities than one person can reasonably manage.

Client communication, scheduling, social media, marketing, invoicing, inventory, emails… the list goes on. This is where a Virtual Assistant (VA) can become your secret weapon.

What Is a Virtual Assistant?

A Virtual Assistant is a remote professional who provides administrative, technical, or creative support. They work from anywhere, no office space needed, and can be hired part-time, full-time, or per project, depending on your needs.

Benefits of a VA for Pet Businesses

 More Time for What Matters Most

Your expertise is in pets; not paperwork. A VA can handle time-consuming tasks like:
- Answering emails and texts
- Scheduling appointmentsConfirming client bookings
- Following up on reviews and inquiries

This frees you to focus on what you do best: caring for pets and growing your business.

☑ Professional Client Communication

Missed messages and inconsistent follow-up can cost you clients. A VA ensures professional, timely communication that strengthens your brand and builds client trust.

☑ Marketing Support

From social media scheduling to writing newsletters, a VA can help you stay visible and relevant online, without the stress of doing it all yourself.

☑ Improved Organization

Need help managing your calendar, updating intake forms, or tracking no-shows? VAs can bring structure to your operations using client management software, spreadsheets, or CRM platforms.

☑ Cost-Effective Help

Hiring a VA is more affordable than hiring a full-time, in-house employee. You only pay for the hours or services you need—no benefits, no payroll taxes, no overhead.

☑ Tasks a VA Can Handle for Pet Pros

- Appointment scheduling & confirmations
- Responding to client inquiries
- Social media posting & engagement
- Email marketing & newsletters
- Invoicing & payment follow-up
- Data entry & form management
- Creating digital flyers or basic graphics
- Online store/product support

When Should You Hire a VA?

★ You're working long hours and still falling behind
★ Client communication is slipping through the cracks
★ You're ready to grow but can't take on more without help
★ You want to scale but not hire full-time staff
★ You're exhausted from trying to "do it all"

Hiring a Virtual Assistant isn't a luxury: it's a smart business move. With the right support, you can reclaim your time, reduce your stress, and focus on building a pet business you truly love.

"This book is a truly practical guide that redefines the grooming process. I found the idea that all parts of the grooming system are interconnected to be incredibly valuable, emphasizing that each step is dependent on the others and not just a series of separate functions. The author, Mary Oquendo, demonstrates this concept through various scenarios, showing how a proactive and holistic approach creates a more resilient business. I would highly recommend this guide to any groomer, whether they are new to the field or a seasoned professional, and whether they work in a salon or mobile setting. This guide is for anyone who wants to take a more holistic, mindful, and gentle approach to grooming. It's a game-changer for the industry, helping groomers not just survive, but truly thrive". -
Anjie Coates, Pawsitive Educational Training

What Immediate Changes Can You Make For This Layer

What Needs To Be Created For This Layer

- Emergency And Disaster Manual
- Standard Operating Manual
- Employee Manual
- Maintenance Schedules
- Set Up Employee Compensation and Pricing Structure
- Employees Surveys And Scheduled Meetings
- Sanitation Schedules
- Network List With Area Professionals
- Supply And Inventory Lists
- Interview Scheduling And Financial Software
- Contact Local Community Organizations That Align With Your Business

Continuing Education

Chapter Seven

Marketing

The Foundation of Successful Marketing

The first rule of successful marketing is simple: offer services you genuinely believe in, and train your team to confidently communicate the value of those services to your clients.

Why Relationships Matter in Marketing

In today's market, success goes beyond offering a great service. It's about building trust, loyalty, and long-term value. Here's why relationship-building is essential to your marketing strategy:

- 1. Trust Drives Sales
    People buy from businesses they trust. When a relationship is in place, clients are more likely to:
    - ❖ Choose you over a competitor.
    - ❖ Accept your professional recommendations.
    - ❖ Forgive occasional mistakes.

- 2. Retention Is More Profitable
    It costs far less to retain a client than to acquire a new one. Strong relationships lead to:
    - ❖ Repeat business.
    - ❖ Higher lifetime value.
    - ❖ More consistent income.

- 3. Referrals and Word-of-Mouth
    Loyal clients become your unpaid marketing team:
    - ❖ They refer their friends and family.
    - ❖ Leave glowing reviews.
    - ❖ Advocate for you in-person and online.

✅ **4. Stand Out in a Competitive Market**
In saturated industries like grooming or coaching, relationships make you unforgettable:
- ❖ Clients remain loyal—even if others are cheaper.
- ❖ They feel emotionally invested in your brand.
- ❖ Your service becomes irreplaceable.

✅ **5. Honest Feedback and Insights**
Connected clients provide valuable feedback:
- ❖ What's working?
- ❖ What's not?
- ❖ What else do they want from you?
- ❖ Use this to refine your services and messaging.

✅ **6. Emotional Connection = Higher Perceived Value**
People buy based on emotion, not just logic. A strong relationship means:
- ❖ Your brand becomes part of their lifestyle.
- ❖ Services feel like a partnership, not a transaction.
- ❖ You create lasting stories, not just one-time sales.

✅ **7. Authentic, Easier Marketing**
When you know your audience:
- ❖ You speak their language.
- ❖ Address their real needs.
- ❖ Your messaging feels personal, not pushy.

💬 "People don't do business with companies. They do business with people they know, like, and trust."

Relationship marketing is no longer optional: it's essential.

How to Market a Service-Based Business

You're not just selling a service, you're selling a result, experience, or transformation. Here's how to do it effectively:

☑ 1. Clarify Your Offer
Be crystal clear about:
- Who you serve.
- What problem you solve.
- The result you deliver.
- What makes your service different.

🔍 Instead of "I'm a pet groomer," try: "I help anxious pets feel safe and loved during grooming using holistic, fear-free techniques."

☑ 2. Build a Strong Online Presence
- A professional website with clear service info, testimonials, and booking options.
- Google Business Profile to appear in local search.
- Active social media accounts where your clients already hang out.

☑ 3. Use Content Marketing
Educate and engage—don't just sell:
- Share tips, how-tos, behind-the-scenes content.
- Write blog posts or create short videos.
- Answer common questions to overcome objections.

📌 Example: "3 Signs Your Pet Might Benefit From a Holistic Groomer"

✅ 4. Showcase Reviews & Testimonials
- Gather Google, Yelp, or Facebook reviews.
- Highlight client success stories.
- Use direct quotes in your social posts and materials.

💬 A happy client's words are more powerful than any ad.

✅ 5. Offer Value Before the Sale
Build trust before asking for money:
- Free consultations.
- Downloadable resources or checklists.
- Email newsletters and live Q&A sessions.

✅ 6. Create Referral & Loyalty Programs
- Offer discounts or perks for client referrals.
- Reward returning clients with exclusive benefits.
- Partner with complementary businesses (trainers, pet sitters, etc.)

✅ 7. Use Email Marketing
Stay top of mind with your audience:
- Share updates, tips, promotions.
- Segment your list for personalized messages.
- Prioritize value over constant selling.

✅ 8. Highlight the Transformation
Don't sell the service—sell the result.
- "I help pet owners feel confident in their pet's care."
- "I help dogs feel comfortable and owners feel proud."

✅ 9. Build Your Network
Build relationships outside your client base:

- Attend local business groups, expos, or trade shows.
- Join online communities.
- Connect with others in your industry.

☑ 10. Be Consistent

Marketing is not a one-time task:
- Post content weekly.
- Send monthly emails.
- Run seasonal promotions.
- Regularly follow up with past clients.

◎ Additional Tools to Amplify Your Marketing

☑ 1. Surveys – Listen and Adapt

- Ask for post-service feedback.
- Learn what services or hours clients want.
- Use standout feedback as testimonials.

"97% of clients say they'd recommend us to a friend!"

☑ 2. Press Releases – Share Your Wins

- Launching a new service?
- Hosting an event or earning a certification?
- Partnering with a local business?

Send a press release to media outlets, then repurpose it for social media and newsletters.

☑ 3. Branded Attire – Wear Your Brand

- Creates a professional, trustworthy appearance.
- Makes your brand recognizable at events and in photos.
- Reinforces consistency across your marketing.

☑ 4. Branded Products – Promote Passively

- Magnets, tote bags, pet bandanas, or first aid kits.
- Use them as gifts, giveaways, or part of a referral program.
- Keeps your business in front of clients daily.

☑ 5. Networking – Relationships Build Referrals

- Attend community or professional meetups.
- Follow up with helpful info or small branded gifts.
- Build your reputation as a trusted resource.

🔁 Pro Tip: Combine Strategies for Maximum Impact

Example Launch Plan:

1. Write a press release for your new service.
2. Host a launch party with branded attire and giveaways.
3. Invite clients, partners, and media contacts.
4. Use surveys to collect feedback and testimonials after.
5. Share it all across your email and social channels.

What Are Your Marketing Ideas

What Are Your Marketing Ideas

Continuing Education

Chapter Eight

Recap

You can absolutely enjoy the rewards of your hard work while effectively managing the challenges that come with success. However, if you continuously deplete your resources without proper oversight, it can eventually lead to critical system failures.

To prevent this, it's essential to protect and maintain the integrity of your foundational structures. This can be achieved through a combination of proactive strategies:

🐾 Regular check-in meetings help ensure that everyone is aligned, and potential issues are addressed before they escalate.

🐾 Client surveys provide valuable insight into satisfaction levels and expectations, allowing you to make informed improvements.

🐾 Maintenance reports keep your operations running efficiently by identifying small problems before they become major disruptions.

🐾 Financial assessments are key to monitoring your budget, managing expenses, and securing the long-term sustainability of your business.

Equally important is prioritizing the well-being of both your team and your clients. Fostering a positive and supportive environment contributes to retention, morale, and overall business health.

With the right systems in place, you truly can have your cake and eat it too.

Chapter Nine

Recommendations

I don't make recommendations lightly in this book.

Every suggestion comes from personal experience or direct knowledge. That's not to say there aren't other, or even better, options out there. I'm simply not personally familiar with them. Please do your own research and make an informed decision.

After this book is initially published, a holistic pet first aid kit will be available at www.SpiritedDog.com.

Below is contact information for people and/or products that I recommend:

Anjie Coates - Anjie Coates offers education for groomers on Pawsitive Educational Training at www.pawsitiveeducationaltraining.com. In addition to online classes and monthly summits for members and nonmembers, she also offers à la carte courses from many educators.

When she's not working toward educating the grooming community, she offers private coaching, pet industry-focused website design, tailor-made operating manuals, and sanitation protocols for your salon or mobile unit. To contact her, just email anjiecoates@gmail.com

Chris Anthony - Chris offers classes and coaching on understanding grooming ergonomics, housecall grooming, avoiding burnout, and dealing with the often-ignored grief in losing our beloved grooming clients.
Chrisbearanthony@gmail.com

Denise Heroux - Denise inspires groomers and business owners to dream bigger, work smarter, and achieve more. With an ambitious spirit, she uses education, leadership, and proven business strategies to create a space where goals aren't just imagined—they're attained. Info@theambitiousgroomer.com

Ashley Hanvey- Ashley Hanvey teaches courses for the modern grooming professional that centers around a respect-centered handling approach. Creator of the class "Don't Grab the Beard!" She teaches alternative handling techniques that help professionals better connect to the dogs on their tables.

Do you have questions or would you like to learn more? Her free introductory class, "Dogs are more than Hair," is available on her website thatscrumptiouspooch.com/. www.respectcenteredhandling.com or ashley@thatscrumptiouspooch.com

Evolution Shears - Evolution Shears was created by groomers for groomers and is designed to work with the anatomy of our hands to prevent repetitive motion injuries such as carpal tunnel. These fully adjustable shears align perfectly with your hands' natural movements and are the most ergonomic grooming shears available.
www.evolutionshears.com

All For Groomers - Every product we create is designed with the groomer's health in mind, offering ergonomic support that protects the back, neck, shoulders, hands, and wrists from strain. At the same time, our tools keep pets safer and more comfortable with restraints that avoid choking or harmful

pressure, while the Groomers Wall helps reduce stress by keeping them calm and gently contained.
www.allforgroomers.com

Michelle Knowles - Discover the innovative techniques and holistic approach offered by All Things Paw and The Herbal Paw Apothecary, an online store founded by Michelle Knowles. Elevate your pet grooming expertise with their comprehensive education and scientifically-backed products, ensuring optimal skin and coat health for every animal in your care
www.allthingspaw.com or Michelle@allthingspaw.com

River Lee - River Lee helps pet grooming professionals transform their businesses by teaching them how to master money, set healthy boundaries, and price with confidence. Through Savvy Groomer, she provides education and tools that empower groomers to create sustainable businesses that support both their financial goals and personal happiness.
Savvygroomer@gmail.com

Amanda McGrath - Amanda helps professional groomers take control of their business through practical tools for organization and time management. She also guides groomers in building thriving home-based salons with confidence and clarity. Pinelaneconsulting@gmail.com or 330-978-1808

Lisa Menze - Lisa Menze, a Nationally Certified Master Groomer, founded Internet Staffing Solutions to help pet care professionals overcome staffing challenges. Through her company, she provides Pet Care Virtual Assistants who are trained to support the unique needs of businesses across the pet care industry. www.internetstaffingsolutions.com

Samantha Palya - As the Enrichment Stylist I teach how to enhance the grooming experience for a pet physically, emotionally, and mentally through relationship building techniques. I also offer business coaching to pet care businesses and industry brands at all stages of their business. I focus on relationship building in business with clients, employees, and business owner mindset.
theenrichmentstylist@gmail.com

Melissa Jepson - Respected speaker Melissa Jepson is dedicated to delivering insightful, relatable content on a broad range of topics relevant to today's grooming professionals. While she has a particular passion for mental health and animal behavior/handling, she strives to provide well-rounded, comprehensive education across the industry.
Melissa@pupsscalepetsalon.com

Mindy Dinwiddie - Mindy Dinwiddie empowers professional groomers through hands-on education, specializing in geriatric pet grooming, branding, and business growth. She inspires groomers to build confidence, skill, and long-term success in their careers. Mindy.Dinwiddie@gmail.com

Candace D'Agnolo - We're not just another pet business coaching program—we're a community where passion meets profit and "pet people" become business pros. NO generic advice. Just real, proven strategies from people who understand your niche's daily challenges. www.PetBossNation.com

Mary Kniskern - Mary Kniskern has dedicated the last decade to helping dogs learn to trust the grooming process. Using Positive Reinforcement techniques in the grooming environment, she's helped many dogs and their families trust the grooming experience. Sonnysspaw@gmail.com or 408-415-7576

Dr. Sacheen Mobley - Making the editing/writing of your projects less painful and more productive. Editing, proofreading, and writing services. support@sacheenmobley.com

Christein Sertzel - Offer a 14-hour credentialed certification program, the Certified Canine Esthetician course, to encourage stylists to think about their ability to provide truly supportive services for pet clients and their owners. This in depth program is designed to teach pet groomers and stylists of all skill levels the foundational information about how canine skin, hair, and coat works, and of how we can best care for optimal pet health within our professional businesses.

For more information, visit www.CanineEsthetician.com

Malissa Conti-Diener - Offers classes in adjunct pet grooming therapies: Massage, Aromatherapy, Acupressure, Energy Healing, Crystal Healing, and Transitional Therapy. For more information, go to www.GetGroomified.com or call 602-573-8329

Barbara Bird - This is the book that every professional groomer should have. The Beyond Suds digital copy is available by emailing Barbara at barbara@thegroompod.com

Dr. Cliff Faver - Offers programs in skin and coat.
https://www.facebook.com/IvSanBernardUS

Come join us in a private Facebook discussion group.

Click the link or scan the code!

www.facebook.com/groups/holisticpetgroomingsystem/

www.ingramcontent.com/pod-product-compliance
Lightning Source LLC
Chambersburg PA
CBHW061821290426
44110CB00027B/2933